Choose Love

STORMIE OMARTIAN

HARVEST HOUSE PUBLISHERS
EUGENE, OREGON

Cover by Harvest House Publishers, Inc., Eugene, Oregon

Back cover author photo © Michael Gomez Photography

CHOOSE LOVE PRAYER AND STUDY GUIDE

Copyright © 2014 by Stormie Omartian
Published by Harvest House Publishers
Eugene, Oregon 97402
www.harvesthousepublishers.com

ISBN 978-0-7369-5993-3 (pbk.)
ISBN 978-0-7369-5994-0 (eBook)

Printed in the United States of America

14 15 16 17 18 19 20 21 / BP-JH / 10 9 8 7 6 5 4 3 2 1

This book belongs to

_____

Please do not read beyond this page
without permission of the person named above.

A supplemental workbook to

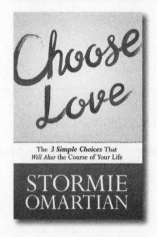

Contents

Third Choice
Choose to Love Others in a Way That Pleases God

What Do I Need Before I Start?

⌒⌒⌒⌒⌒⌒⌒⌒⌒⌒⌒⌒⌒⌒⌒⌒⌒⌒⌒⌒⌒⌒⌒⌒⌒⌒⌒⌒

This *Prayer and Study Guide* is a companion to the book *Choose Love*. So you will need to have that book with you in order to answer the questions and follow the instructions after you've read each chapter (it will be referred to as "the book" within each week's questions and directions). You will also need a Bible to read the suggested Scriptures and write out your prayers and personal insights. I have used the New King James Version here, but you can use the translation you are most comfortable reading. I also recommend having a small notebook or journal with you because I believe you will want to write more than space allows for in some of the questions.

The purpose of this *Prayer and Study Guide* is to convince you of how much God loves you and to encourage the deepening of your relationship with Him. It will also help you grow in love for the Lord and effectively express your love to Him. It will then show how God wants to guide you as you extend His love to others, and what needs to be determined first by seeking God's will and discerning His instructions in specific situations. The more you understand how much God loves you, the more you will love Him, and the more He will pour His love into you so you can better love others. In the process, the course of your life will be altered for the better. That's because God wants to bless you in ways you may not have realized before, and that only happens as you show love for others.

This *Prayer and Study Guide* is not intended to just give you something to do or to be busywork for you. This is not like being in school where you fill out papers for a grade. No one is judging you. What you write on these pages is for the purpose of helping you draw conclusions and make decisions based on biblical truth and the evidence of your own life experiences.

In Private or Group Study

You may choose to complete this *Prayer and Study Guide* by yourself—between just you and God—and He will speak to your heart as you ask Him to do so.

However, you may also want to get together with one or more other people in a group setting, which is also extremely valuable and uplifting. If so, read the chapter (or chapters) in the book assigned for that week, depending on how many chapters your group has decided to cover in a week. If your group wants to do one chapter a week, it will take approximately five months of meeting together once a week. Or, if you and the others have the time to cover two chapters a week, you will be done in about three months. You decide how you want to do it.

One of the advantages of doing this *Prayer and Study Guide* as a group—or even with just one other person—is that you can share your answers with others as you feel led. This book is personal for you, so only share what you are comfortable doing and keep private what you want to keep private. No one else should ever be reading your *Prayer and Study Guide* unless granted permission by you. Just know that what you do share with others from an open heart can bring great encouragement, healing, and blessings not only for them but for you as well.

Usually, more people will be wanting to share than there is time for, so decide how much time to allow for your meeting—anywhere from one to two hours is good—and try to abide by that. Busy people tend to drop out when they can't depend on meetings letting out at the agreed upon time.

After going through the questions, ask for a few testimonies of what God taught or revealed to each person—about Him or about themselves—or how He encouraged them as they read the chapter and responded to the questions.

Always close the meeting with a prayer. Whatever way God leads you in this—whether *you* pray, or you call upon several to pray, or let whoever feels led to pray—will be a very powerful time for everyone.

I pray that as you complete this *Prayer and Study Guide*, you will meet God in His Word and it will be life-changing for you. I pray you will grow in greater appreciation of God's love for you, your love for Him, and the love He puts in your heart for others.

When You Are Finished

Once you have completed this *Prayer and Study Guide*, you will have written prayers you can pray again and again. You will have recorded insights the Lord has given you regarding specific Scriptures. And you will also have written Scripture out as prayers and be more accustomed to including God's Word in your prayers. In this way, this *Prayer and Study Guide* will be a powerful tool to help ignite your prayer life, keep you refreshed and renewed, and enhance your ability to choose to receive God's love for you, express your love for Him, and love others in a way that pleases Him every day.

When you do this, you will be amazed at what doors will open up for you in your personal life—doors to greater fulfillment, positive experiences with other people, and a sense of the Lord's love with you always. Your love will grow for God every time you express it to Him, and He will pour more of His love, mercy, and compassion into you. You will not only know Him better, but you will know yourself better as well. And you will have a greater sense of His purpose for your life.

Shall we get started?

First Choice

Choose to Receive God's *Love* for You

Week One

Read Chapter 1:
"See Yourself the Way God Sees You"
in *Choose Love*

~~~~~~

1. Are you generally hard on yourself or fairly forgiving? Do you have extremely high standards and require perfection from yourself, or do you give yourself grace enough to say without condemnation, "I will simply try harder in that area"? The difference is whether you beat yourself up when you feel you have not lived up to your own standards or not. Explain your answer.

    _____

    _____

    _____

    _____

2. Do you see any weakness in yourself as failure on your part or as an opportunity to trust God to be strong in you?

    _____

    _____

    _____

In light of your answer, write out a prayer asking God to help you see any failure you feel you have experienced as an opportunity for Him to be strong in you. If you can think of a particular time in your past where you should have turned to Him for strength and didn't, be specific about that.

_____

_____

_____

_____

Is there an incident in your memory that you think of as a failure on your part and you are still upset by it? If so, write out a prayer asking God to heal that memory and enable you to forgive yourself. If you have no such memory, write out a prayer asking God to show you if there is anything at all from your past that still causes you to cringe when you think of it, and ask God to heal that memory completely.

_____

_____

_____

_____

3. Do you ever allow the opinions of others to influence the opinion you have of yourself? Explain.

_____

_____

_____

_____

4. Do you ever scrutinize yourself and your life in such a way that it's as though you are looking through a magnifying mirror where every flaw is clearly seen? Explain your answer.

_____

_____

_____

_____

Write out a prayer asking God to help you see yourself as *He* sees you and not through the critical eyes of others.

_____

_____

_____

_____

5. Read 2 Peter 1:2-4. What has given us all things that pertain to life and godliness? (verses 2-3)

_____

_____

_____

_____

What else have we been given? (verse 4)

_____

_____

_____

Why has God given us these great promises? (verse 4)

_____

_____

_____

_____

What is the good news in these verses for you personally? Write out your answer as a prayer. (For example, "Thank You, Lord, that Your divine power has given us all things that pertain to...")

_____

_____

_____

_____

6. What is the first way you must choose love in order to see your life change? (See page 15 in the book, the first paragraph under "Three Simple Choices That Will Alter the Course of Your Life.") Write out your answer as a prayer asking God to help you make that choice every day.

_____

_____

_____

_____

7. What is the second way you must choose love in order to see great blessings in your life? (See page 15 in the book, the last

paragraph.) Write out your answer as a prayer asking God to help you make that choice every day.

_____

_____

_____

_____

8. What is the third way you must choose love in order to alter the course of your life for the better? (See page 16 in the book, first paragraph.) Write out your answer as a prayer asking God to help you make that choice every day.

_____

_____

_____

_____

9. Do you believe God loves you? How strongly or consistently do you feel His love toward you? Tell Him what you would like to see happen in the future regarding your sense of being loved by Him. Write out your answer as a prayer. (For example, "Lord, help me to understand Your love for me in a way that…")

_____

_____

_____

_____

Read Job 7:17. Do you ever have that same thought Job had? Do you sometimes wonder if God values you or *why* He values you? Do you ever feel you are not valuable to Him? Explain why or why not.

_____

_____

_____

10. Pray the prayer on page 18 in the book. Write out several sentences from the prayer that are especially important to you right now. You can write them in the exact words used there or in your own words.

_____

_____

_____

_____

Week Two

Read Chapter 2:
"Understand Who God Really Is"
in *Choose Love*

~~~~~~

1. Read page 23 in the book, the last two paragraphs before "Some Things You Should Know About God." Why is knowing God and understanding who He really is important?

   _____

   _____

   _____

   _____

2. What is your view of God? Describe what you see in your mind when you think of Him. How do you personally feel about Him? Do you think of Him as distant or close? Friendly or stern? Loving or critical? Be completely honest with yourself. No one is testing you or checking your answers.

   _____

   _____

   _____

   _____

3. Read the following Scriptures. Under each one write what they say about God. (See also pages 23-25 under "Some Things You Must Know About God.")

Psalm 90:1-2

_____

_____

Genesis 1:26

_____

_____

Psalm 146:8

_____

_____

John 14:10-11

_____

_____

1 Chronicles 16:34

_____

_____

1 John 4:16

_____

_____

2 Corinthians 6:18

_____

_____

Psalm 33:5

_____

_____

4. Read the section of text under "God, the Creator of Everything, Did Not Create Evil" on pages 27-28 in the book. If God did not create evil, where did evil come from? What *did* God create in Lucifer? What did Lucifer become and why?

_____

_____

_____

_____

5. Read the first paragraph on page 29 in the book. In light of that information, why do we need to know God well?

_____

_____

_____

_____

6. Read Psalm 139:13-16. (See also the third paragraph on page 29 in the book.) What do these verses say about you? What is true of you? Write out your answer as a prayer of thanksgiving

to God. (For example, "Lord, I thank You that You saw me as I was growing in my mother's womb, and...")

_____

_____

_____

_____

7. Read page 30, fourth paragraph, in the book. God is everywhere, but where will you find the greatest manifestation of His love and power?

_____

_____

Write out a prayer inviting God to be in your life in a powerful way and to help you see His love for you in ways you have not previously seen or understood.

_____

_____

_____

_____

8. Read Psalm 29:2 and Hebrews 13:8. In light of these two Scriptures, what is true about God? (See also pages 32 and 33 in the book.)

_____

_____

_____

_____

9. Read Psalm 68:34-35. What does God give to His people? Do
    you believe He gives that to you? Why or why not?

_____

_____

_____

_____

Write out a prayer thanking God that nothing is impossible for
Him where you are concerned.

_____

_____

_____

Read Psalm 50:10-12 and Matthew 6:8. Also read page 35, the
first three paragraphs. If God owns everything and knows what
you need, do you believe He can provide for you when you ask
Him to do so? Why or why not?

_____

_____

_____

_____

Read Psalm 56:8. (See also page 35, the last three paragraphs, in the book.) Do you believe God sees you at all times—not just to keep track of your mistakes, but to watch over you because He loves you?

_____

_____

_____

_____

Write out a prayer thanking God that His Word says He sees you and knows the circumstances of your life. Ask Him to increase your faith in His ability to watch over you.

_____

_____

_____

_____

10. Pray the prayer on page 36 in the book. Write out several sentences from the prayer that are especially important to you right now. You can write them in the exact words used there or in your own words.

_____

_____

_____

_____

Week Three

Read Chapter 3:
"Receive All God Has for You"
in *Choose Love*

~~~~~~

1. Read Luke 1:31 and Matthew 1:23. (Also see page 40, the last paragraph.) What was God's greatest gift of all—His Son—to be called, and what did these two names mean?

   _____

   _____

   _____

   _____

   What do those two names of Jesus and their meaning signify to you?

   _____

   _____

   _____

   _____

2. Read the following Scriptures. Under each one write the name
    Jesus is referred to as being.

    John 1:1-2,14

    _____

    _____

    John 1:29

    _____

    _____

    John 6:48-51

    _____

    _____

    John 10:9

    _____

    _____

    John 10:11

    _____

    _____

    John 14:6

    _____

    _____

3. Read Proverbs 20:9. Do you believe you are able to purify your-self from sin and make your own heart clean? Why or why not?

_____

_____

Read Romans 5:19. The disobedient man is Adam. The obe-dient Man is Jesus. Can we make ourselves righteous? Why or why not?

_____

_____

Read John 14:6 again. Why can't we get to God on our own?

_____

_____

4. Read the section of the book under "Jesus Is Called Savior, Redeemer, and Restorer" on page 46. Why is Jesus called Savior?

_____

_____

_____

_____

Why is Jesus called Redeemer?

_____

_____

_____

_____

Why is Jesus called the Restorer?

_____

_____

_____

_____

5. Read 1 Corinthians 3:11. (See also page 47, last two paragraphs.) When you receive Jesus, what do you receive?

    _____

    _____

    _____

    Have you received Jesus? Do you feel you have received a foundation in Him? Explain why or why not.

    _____

    _____

    _____

    In light of your answer above, write out a prayer asking Jesus to help you to build on the new foundation you are given in Him.

    _____

    _____

    _____

    _____

6. When we receive Jesus, what does He share with us? (See page
    49, first two paragraphs.)

    _____

    _____

Jesus and the Holy Spirit are the two greatest manifestations of
God's love for us. Read the following Scriptures. Under each
one write what it says about the Holy Spirit.

John 14:26

_____

_____

1 Corinthians 2:11-12

_____

_____

1 Corinthians 12:3

_____

_____

Ephesians 1:13-14

_____

_____

Romans 8:9

_____

_____

1 John 4:13

_____

_____

2 Corinthians 3:17

_____

_____

7. In light of the Scriptures above, how is God's Holy Spirit one
    of God's greatest gifts of love to you along with Jesus and His
    Word?

    _____

    _____

    _____

    _____

8. Read the following Scriptures. Under each one write what we
    receive when we receive Jesus.

    John 3:13-15

    _____

    _____

    John 5:39-40

    _____

    _____

1 Corinthians 8:6

_____

_____

John 10:27-30

_____

_____

2 Corinthians 5:21

_____

_____

John 6:27

_____

_____

John 6:37

_____

_____

9. Read the following Scriptures. Under each write what Jesus does or has done.

John 1:18

_____

_____

John 3:35-36

_____

_____

John 6:44

_____

_____

John 10:17-18

_____

_____

John 12:44-45

_____

_____

John 12:47-49

_____

_____

10. Pray the prayer on page 56 in the book. Write out several sentences from the prayer that are especially important to you right now. You can write them in the exact words used there or in your own words.

_____

_____

_____

_____

Week Four

Read Chapter 4:
"Read God's Love Letter to You"
in *Choose Love*

〰〰〰〰〰〰〰〰〰〰〰〰〰〰〰〰〰〰〰〰〰〰〰〰

1. What do you believe about God's Word? Have you tended to think of it as a list of dos and don'ts, or do you believe it shows God's living way to make life work? Explain.

    _____

    _____

    _____

    _____

2. Given that the entire Bible is God's love letter to us, Psalm 119 is specifically a love letter to God about His Word. The path to happiness is doing God's will according to His Word. Read the following verses. Under each one describe what happens to those who read and keep God's Word.

    Psalm 119:1-4

    _____

    _____

Psalm 119:10-12

_____

_____

Psalm 119:97-99

_____

_____

Psalm 119:105-107

_____

_____

Psalm 119:129-130

_____

_____

Psalm 119:143-144

_____

_____

Psalm 119:159-162

_____

_____

Psalm 119:165-167

_____

_____

3. Read the following Scriptures. Under each one describe what happens to those who don't keep God's Word.

Psalm 119:5-6

_____

_____

Psalm 119:36-37

_____

_____

Psalm 119:67

_____

_____

Psalm 119:92-93

_____

_____

Psalm 119:133-134

_____

_____

4. In light of the Scriptures in Psalm 119 above, write out a prayer of thanksgiving to God for His Word—His love letter to you. Include what you are most thankful for regarding it.

_____

_____

_____

_____

5. Read 2 Timothy 3:16-17. Do you believe all Scripture has been
    given to us by inspiration of God? Why or why not? Why do
    we need His Word?

_____

_____

_____

_____

6. Read Isaiah 55:10-11. (See also page 69 in the book.) What do
    these verses say to you about God's Word and His ways? How
    does God's Word compare to rain?

_____

_____

_____

_____

7. Read Psalm 1:1-6. In light of these verses, how can you be
    blessed? (verses 1-2)

_____

_____

_____

_____

What happens to you when you love God's Word and read it often? (verse 3)

_____

_____

_____

_____

What happens to those who do not read or love God's Word? What happens when the storms of life blow turbulence into their lives? (verses 4-6)

_____

_____

_____

_____

8. Read Hebrews 4:12. How is God's Word described in this verse? Write out your answer as a prayer of thanks to God for His Word. (For example, "Thank You, Lord, that Your Word is always active and alive in my life when I read it and keep it in my heart...")

_____

_____

_____

_____

9. Read Proverbs 28:9 and John 15:7. In light of these verses, how
   important is God's Word to our prayer life and to establishing
   our relationship with God?

   _____

   _____

   _____

   _____

10. Read the prayer on page 68 in the book. Write out several sen-
    tences from the prayer that are especially important to you right
    now. You can write them in the exact words used there or in
    your own words.

    _____

    _____

    _____

    _____

Week Five

Read Chapter 5:
"Accept God's Grace and Mercy"
in *Choose Love*

~~~~~~

1. Read Ephesians 2:8. In light of this Scripture, can you save yourself? Why or why not?

   _____

   _____

   _____

   _____

2. What is grace? (See page 72, the section of text below "Understanding God's Grace.")

   _____

   _____

   _____

   _____

Read Hebrews 4:16. Write out this verse as a prayer. (For example, "Lord, help me to come boldly before…")

_____

_____

_____

_____

Describe one of the most important ways you have seen God's grace extended toward you.

_____

_____

_____

_____

3. Read Romans 3:21-26. Don't let Paul's two extremely long sentences, with a lot of information in them, intimidate you because it's good to have the context of what he is talking about to the Romans. Focus on verses 23-24 and answer the following questions: Who of us have sinned and fallen short of God's glory? How have we been rescued?

_____

_____

_____

_____

4. Read Ephesians 1:3-6. This is another of Paul's very long sentences, this time to the Ephesians. What is the truth in what he teaches that describes what God's grace has done for you?

_____

_____

_____

_____

5. Read Titus 3:4-7. What is the most important way God's mercy has manifested toward us who believe in Him?

_____

_____

_____

_____

6. Read the following Scriptures. Under each one write what is true of God's mercy toward you.

Lamentations 3:22-23

_____

_____

Psalm 103:11-12

_____

_____

Ephesians 2:4-6

_____

_____

Psalm 86:5

_____

_____

1 Peter 1:3

_____

_____

Titus 3:4-7

_____

_____

7. Describe God's mercy. (See page 73 in the book, the section of
   text below "Understanding God's Mercy.")

_____

_____

_____

_____

8. Read Psalm 23. Under each of the verses below, write what God
   has for you when you make Him your Lord. Write out your
   answer as a prayer. (For example in verse 1, "Lord, thank You

that because You are my Lord and Shepherd, You will provide for me…")

Verse 1

_____

_____

Verse 2

_____

_____

Verse 3

_____

_____

Verse 4

_____

_____

Verse 5

_____

_____

Verse 6

_____

_____

9. Read Hebrews 8:12. In what most important way does God show His mercy toward you every day? How grateful are you to Him for that? Write out your answer as a prayer to God. (For example, "Lord, thank You that You show mercy to me by forgiving my sins so completely that...")

_____

_____

_____

_____

10. Pray the prayer on page 83 in the book. Write out several sentences from the prayer that are especially important to you right now. You can write them in the exact words used there or in your own words.

_____

_____

_____

_____

Week Six

Read Chapter 6:
"Recognize the Ways God Loves You"
in *Choose Love*

∿∿∿∿∿∿∿∿∿∿∿∿∿∿∿∿∿∿∿∿∿∿∿∿∿∿∿∿∿∿∿∿

1. Everything we do in life that has eternal value hinges on two
    things: loving God and loving others. We love God because He
    first loved us. If we don't understand how much He loves us, we
    won't love Him as much as we should and can't love others in
    the way He wants us to. Read the following Scriptures. Under
    each one write what it says about God's love.

    Psalm 17:7

    _____

    _____

    Jeremiah 31:3

    _____

    _____

    Revelation 3:20

    _____

    _____

1 John 4:13

_____

_____

2 Corinthians 1:9-10

_____

_____

John 10:10

_____

_____

John 14:2-3

_____

_____

2. In light of the Scriptures above, write out a prayer thanking God for all the ways He shows His love toward you.

_____

_____

_____

_____

3. Read 1 John 4:15-18. How do you know God lives in you and you in Him? (verse 15)

_____

_____

_____

_____

What happens when you invite God to live in you, and why does that happen? (verse 16)

_____

_____

_____

_____

When you receive God's perfect love, what happens? What does God's perfect love in you accomplish? (verse 17)

_____

_____

_____

_____

What does fear do to you? What does living in fear *say* about someone? (verse 18)

_____

_____

_____

_____

4. Read 1 John 4:19. What do we have to understand in order to love God? Write out your answer as a prayer to Him. (For example, "Lord, thank You that You first...")

_____

_____

_____

_____

5. After all that God had done for the Israelites, they still questioned Him. "'I have loved you,' says the LORD. 'Yet you say, "In what way have You loved us?"'" (Malachi 1:2). They did not recognize all He had done and was doing for them. Write out a prayer of thanksgiving to God for the ways He has shown His love to you that you have not thanked Him for before or need to thank Him for again.

_____

_____

_____

_____

6. Read the following Scriptures. Under each one write how God's love is shown toward you.

    James 1:5

_____

_____

2 Timothy 3:16

_____

_____

1 Corinthians 2:9-10

_____

_____

Isaiah 30:21

_____

_____

Psalm 94:14

_____

_____

Romans 8:32

_____

_____

Revelation 21:6

_____

_____

7. In light of the Scriptures above, write out a prayer thanking God for all the ways He shows His love toward you.

    _____

    _____

    _____

    _____

8. Read the following Scriptures. Under each one write out a short prayer thanking God for His love toward you shown in that promise.

    Psalm 147:3

    _____

    _____

    Isaiah 44:3

    _____

    _____

    Proverbs 3:6

    _____

    _____

    Deuteronomy 20:4

    _____

    _____

Psalm 138:8

_____

_____

Psalm 89:3

_____

_____

9. In light of the Scriptures above, write out a prayer thanking God
   for all the ways He shows His love toward you.

   _____

   _____

   _____

   _____

10. Pray the prayer on page 95 in the book. Write out several sen-
    tences from the prayer that are especially important to you right
    now. You can write them in the exact words used there or in
    your own words.

    _____

    _____

    _____

    _____

Week Seven

Read Chapter 7:
"Know What God's Love Will Do in Your Life"
in *Choose Love*

～～～～～～～～～～～～～～～～～～～～～～～～～～～～～～～～

1. What do you feel in your heart right now about how much God loves you? Write out your answer as a prayer to God. (For example, "Lord, I have a hard time trusting that You really love me. I know You are the God of love, so I pray You will help me to…") (Or pray, "Lord, I sense Your love for me every day, and I pray You will show me any way I don't fully trust You in that regard. Help me to…")

   _____

   _____

   _____

   _____

2. In light of your prayer above, in what way did you feel, or *not* feel, loved in your past? Explain.

   _____

   _____

   _____

   _____

Do you see any correlation between your experience of feeling loved in your past—or not feeling loved—and how you feel about the love of God toward you today?

_____

_____

_____

_____

3. Read Psalm 107:26-31. Anyone who has ever been in a storm at sea knows how frightening and violent it can be. The waves can be huge and rock the boat in a frightening way. These kinds of storms can cause even the most hardened of hearts to turn to God and pray. Have you ever been in a storm in your own personal life that rocked everything—your health, relationships, foundation, work, sense of well-being, understanding of purpose, etc.? According to these verses, what should you do? And what will God do in response? (verses 28-30)

_____

_____

_____

_____

What should we not forget to do when God calms the storm in our life? (verse 31)

_____

_____

_____

_____

Read Matthew 14:25-32. The disciples of Jesus were in a boat in the middle of the sea when a storm came up with strong winds and waves that tossed their vessel. Then they saw Jesus walking toward them on the water and that made them afraid. When Jesus called Peter to come to Him, Peter walked on water until his fear of the increasing wind caused him to sink. What did Peter do then? (verse 30)

_____

_____

_____

How did Jesus respond to Peter? (verse 31)

_____

_____

_____

What happened when Jesus got into the boat with them? (verse 32)

_____

_____

What did the disciples do then? (verse 33)

_____

_____

_____

In light of what happened with Jesus and His disciples in this storm, what could you do with regard to any storm that happens in your personal life?

_____

_____

_____

What could you say to the Lord? (verse 30)

_____

_____

_____

What should you have in the middle of a storm? What should you *not* have? (verse 31)

_____

_____

_____

What could you invite Jesus to do that He did for His disciples? (verse 32) What difference did this make to them?

_____

_____

_____

When you invite Jesus into the situation with you and He calms the storm, what should you be certain to do? (verse 33)

_____

_____

_____

4. Read Romans 8:28. What is the promise to you in this verse? Do you believe God loves you enough to do that for you if you pray and ask Him to?

    _____

    _____

    _____

    Read Matthew 19:26. (See also the last three paragraphs on page 101 in the book.) How can God bring good out of a seemingly impossible situation?

    _____

    _____

    _____

    Write out a prayer thanking God for the love He has for you, as proved by the specific promises in these two Scriptures.

    _____

    _____

    _____

    _____

5. Read 2 Chronicles 15:1-4. After the Spirit of God came upon
    Azariah, what did he tell King Asa? (verses 1-2)

    _____

    _____

    _____

    _____

    Israel had turned away from God for quite a while, but when
    they turned back to Him, what happened? (verses 3-4)

    _____

    _____

    _____

    _____

    What does this sign of God's great love for them mean for you
    today? How will the nature of God to forgive and receive us
    back always be a sign of His love for you? Write out your answer
    as a prayer of thanks to God. (For example, "Lord, I am grate-
    ful that as long as I am with You, You will be...")

    _____

    _____

    _____

    _____

6. Read Psalm 34:17-19. What must we do in order for the Lord
    to deliver us from all our troubles? Write out your answer as a
    prayer of thanks to God for His love shown to you in this way.

(For example, "Lord, I thank You that when I cry out to You in prayer, You will…")

_____

_____

_____

_____

7. Read Psalm 92:12-15. What does the Scripture say about your future and how much God loves you?

_____

_____

_____

_____

Read John 15:15. What does Jesus call us? What do you think about that? How does that make you feel?

_____

_____

_____

_____

8. Read Ephesians 3:14-21. In this section of Scripture, Paul is praying for the Ephesians. What did he pray God would give them? (verse 16)

_____

_____

_____

Why did Paul want that for them? (verses 17-19)

_____

_____

_____

What is God able to do in us and how does He do it? (verse 20)

_____

_____

_____

In light of these verses, how will God empower you to live the life He has for you?

_____

_____

_____

In light of all you have learned in this chapter, when your life seems overwhelming, what do you need to do? Write out your answer as a prayer. (For example, "Lord, when I feel overwhelmed by my life, help me to remember that You…")

_____

_____

_____

_____

9. Read Psalm 139:1-5. In light of these verses, how well do you feel God knows you? What is your expectation of His love toward you in the future?

_____

_____

_____

_____

After reading this chapter, how can you expect God to show His love toward you in the future?

_____

_____

_____

Do you think it's presumptuous to believe that God will calm the storms in your life and be your hiding place from trouble? Write out a prayer asking Him to help you remember that He loves you enough to do all those things mentioned in the six subheads of this chapter. (See pages 99, 101, 102, 104, 105, and 106 in the book.)

_____

_____

_____

_____

10. Pray the prayer on page 109 in the book. Write out several sentences from the prayer that are especially important to you right now. You can write them in the exact words used there or in your own words.

_____

_____

_____

_____

Second Choice

Choose to Express Your Love for God

Week Eight

Read Chapter 8:
"Love Who He Is Wholeheartedly"
in *Choose Love*

⌐⌐⌐⌐⌐⌐⌐⌐⌐⌐⌐⌐⌐⌐⌐⌐⌐⌐⌐⌐⌐⌐⌐⌐⌐⌐⌐⌐⌐⌐⌐⌐⌐⌐⌐⌐

1. Read Mark 12:30 and Matthew 10:37. Also read page 114 in the book. Describe below the three ways Jesus wants us to love Him.

   _____

   _____

   _____

   _____

2. Read page 115, under "Falling in Love with Someone Special." The last paragraph describes the way it feels to fall in love. Think of a time when you remember most feeling that way about a person, a child, a grandchild, or even a beloved pet who became like a family member. (Many people have never fallen in love with a person because they were not given the opportunity. And pets are faithful gifts from God who provide unconditional love.) The point is not who the object of your love was or is, but

what you felt or feel when you think about this. Describe your greatest sense of feeling love.

_____

_____

_____

_____

Is any part of your experience similar to the description of what love feels like in the last paragraph on page 115? How so?

_____

_____

_____

_____

Do you feel the same way about God, Jesus, and the Holy Spirit as you have described above or as described on page 115? Is your love for God passionate and real? Write out your answers in a prayer asking God to help you love Him the same way you have loved the most important object of your love so far. (For example, "Lord, help me to fully receive Your love and express my love to You in ways that are like…")

_____

_____

_____

_____

3. Read Matthew 6:21. (See page 116, last paragraph.) Do you see God as your greatest treasure? Describe your greatest treasure on earth. Then describe God as being far greater than that. Write out your answer in the form of a prayer. For example, "Lord, my greatest treasure on earth is…(my child, my friend, my husband, my sister, my grandchild, my dog, etc.), and as much as I love that person (pet, place, thing, experience, etc.) I love You even more because You have…(given me…, loved me, touched me, etc.)."

    _____

    _____

    _____

    _____

4. Read Matthew 13:45-46. In this parable Jesus talks about someone finding a valuable pearl and then selling all he has to have it. Jesus said this compares to letting go of everything in order to have the kingdom of heaven. This is about giving up all else for what is most important. The kingdom is valuable because of the King. Write out a prayer asking God to help you give up whatever you need to let go of so He can be first place in your heart. That does not mean you can't have anything else in your life—not at all. This means God wants you to make Him your top priority. (For example, "Lord, help me to never let my own interests take precedence over my interest in You…")

    _____

    _____

    _____

    _____

5. Read Luke 12:15-21. Jesus told this parable about a person who laid up treasure only on earth and not in heaven. To lay up treasure in heaven we must be rich toward God. Again, the point Jesus was making is that God must be our priority—the One we love most. Write out a prayer asking God to help you lay up treasure in heaven in that way.

_____

_____

_____

_____

6. Read Luke 12:34. What determines what we have in our hearts? Write out your answer as a prayer asking God to help you make Him your greatest treasure. Ask Him to show you the truth about where your heart is. (For example, "Lord, I want You to always be my greatest treasure, so I pray You will reveal to me...")

_____

_____

_____

_____

7. Read the following verses. Under each one write what it says about your heart.

1 Samuel 16:7

_____

_____

Romans 5:5

_____

_____

Matthew 5:8

_____

_____

8. Read page 118 in the book. Write out a prayer asking God to
    show you what you can do to make more room in your life for
    Him.

_____

_____

_____

_____

Write down all He shows you, in answer to the above prayer,
about what you can specifically do to make more room for the
Lord in your heart. Whatever He brings to mind about that in
the future, jot it down.

_____

_____

_____

_____

9. Write out a prayer expressing your love for God. Ask Him to help you love Him so much that you are able to express your love for Him in a deeper way than you ever have before.

_____

_____

_____

_____

10. Pray the prayer on page 119 in the book. Write out several sentences from the prayer that are especially important to you right now. You can write them in the exact words used there or in your own words.

_____

_____

_____

_____

Week Nine

Read Chapter 9:
"Live His Way Uncompromisingly"
in *Choose Love*

∼∼∼∼∼∼∼∼∼∼∼∼∼∼∼∼∼∼∼∼∼∼∼∼∼∼∼∼∼∼∼∼∼∼∼∼∼∼∼

1. Read Isaiah 59:1-2. Read page 121 and the first two paragraphs of page 122 in the book. What does any kind of sin do to our relationship with God? How does it affect our prayers?

    _____

    _____

    _____

    _____

2. Read John 14:21-23. What does choosing to live God's way clearly demonstrate about us? How do we show love for God? (See page 125, last two paragraphs.)

    _____

    _____

    _____

    _____

3. Read Psalm 107:17-20. We can never be so deep in sin that God will not hear our prayers of true repentance. Write out a prayer thanking God that He always hears your prayers. Ask Him to show you anything at all of which you need to confess and repent. Don't worry. We all have something in us that falls short of God's glory. Do we doubt God? Do we have a less than perfect attitude? Is there any envy in us that has crept in, much to our surprise? Whatever it is, God will show you when you ask Him. Write down what He shows you.

_____

_____

_____

_____

Read Psalm 90:8. What does this say about our sins with regard to God?

_____

_____

_____

4. Read Psalm 1:1-3 and Psalm 18:23-24. What is the reward of loving God's law? How does the Lord reward us? What do we need to do to receive His reward? Write out your answer as a prayer to God asking Him to help you stay blameless before Him. (For example, "Lord, I thank You that You reward me according to…")

_____

_____

_____

_____

5. Read Psalm 24:3-5. Outward religion means nothing; inward
    holiness means everything. Who can enter into God's presence?
    What do we have to do to experience a deeper sense of the Lord's
    presence?

_____

_____

_____

_____

6. Read the words of Jesus in John 5:42-43. How did Jesus know
    that the men He was talking to did not love God?

_____

_____

_____

_____

7. Read Psalm 139:23-24. See also page 129, the last three com-
    plete paragraphs. We show love for God by asking Him to show
    us anything in our heart that should not be there. Write out this
    prayer of David as a prayer from your heart.

_____

_____

_____

_____

Write out a prayer in your own words asking God to show you if there is anything in your own heart you need to see.

_____

_____

_____

_____

8. Read the following Scriptures. Under each one write what Jesus said about *living in His love*. What do you need to do in order to do that?

John 15:10-11

_____

_____

John 14:24

_____

_____

9. Read the following Scriptures. Under each one write what it says about sin and finding victory over it.

Romans 6:6

_____

_____

Romans 7:19-25

_____

_____

Psalm 119:67-68

_____

_____

Psalm 119:142-143

_____

_____

Proverbs 3:12

_____

_____

10. Pray the prayer on page 132 in the book. Write out several sentences from the prayer that are especially important to you right now. You can write them in the exact words used there or in your own words.

_____

_____

_____

_____

Week Ten

Read Chapter 10:
"Learn to Worship Him Lavishly"
in *Choose Love*

∿∿∿∿∿∿∿∿∿∿∿∿∿∿∿∿∿∿∿∿∿∿∿∿∿

1. Read Psalm 149:6. In light of this Scripture, what should we always do? (A two-edged sword is the Word of God.)

    _____

    _____

    _____

    _____

    Do you find giving God praise and worship every day easy or hard to do? Don't hesitate to give your answer, because many people find praying easy and worshipping hard, while others feel that worship is no problem and praying is more difficult. Do you feel you are where you want to be with regard to expressing your love to God in worship?

    _____

    _____

    _____

    _____

2.   Read Psalm 150:2. What are the two most important things for
     which we should praise God?

     _____

     _____

     _____

     See page 135 in the book, the first three paragraphs. Why is
     praise and worship the purest form of prayer and adoration?

     _____

     _____

     _____

     When we praise God, we are reminded of who He is and what
     He has done. In a few words, write out who God is to you and
     what He has done that you most praise Him for right now. (For
     example, "Lord, I praise You that You are...and You have...")

     _____

     _____

     _____

     Read Psalm 30:4. What are you supposed to do?

     _____

     _____

     _____

3. Read Psalm 108:1-5. Answer the following questions about this psalm of David. Why was David certain he would praise God? (verse 1)

   _____

   _____

   How early in the day would he praise God? (verse 2)

   _____

   _____

   Besides praising God alone, with whom else did he decide to praise God? (verse 3)

   _____

   _____

   For what two things does David specifically praise God? (verse 4)

   _____

   _____

   Over what did David magnify the Lord in praise? (verse 5)

   _____

   _____

   Write out your own prayer of praise to God using the same ideas, but put them in your own words. (For example, "Lord, I am committed to making praise of You a way of life. I will...")

_____

_____

_____

_____

4. Read 2 Chronicles 20:15-22. Jehoshaphat, the king of Judah,
    faced a serious threat from his enemies, but he humbled himself
    before the Lord and called the nation to fast and pray and seek
    God. They knew they had no power against this enemy, but they
    declared their eyes were on God. The Spirit of the Lord came
    upon Jahaziel and spoke through him to Jehoshaphat saying,

    > Listen, all you of Judah and you inhabitants of Jerusa-
    > lem, and you, King Jehoshaphat! Thus says the LORD
    > to you: "Do not be afraid nor dismayed because of this
    > great multitude, for the battle is not yours, but God's."

    Under each verse below, write what great thing God told them
    to do that *we* can also greatly benefit from remembering or
    doing when *we* face an enemy.

    2 Chronicles 20:15

    _____

    _____

    2 Chronicles 20:17

    _____

    _____

2 Chronicles 20:18

_____

_____

2 Chronicles 20:19

_____

_____

2 Chronicles 20:20

_____

_____

2 Chronicles 20:21

_____

_____

2 Chronicles 20:22

_____

_____

5. As a result of Jehoshaphat doing the things he did when faced
    with his greatest threat from an enemy, he and his people expe-
    rienced their greatest victory. What does that inspire you to do
    when *you* experience your greatest threat from an enemy? How
    important is worshipping God?

    _____

    _____

_____

_____

6. Considering your answers in numbers 4 and 5, write out a prayer asking God to help you to remember all of the things Jehoshaphat did before his greatest victory when you are faced with a threat from the enemy. Ask God to help you learn to praise and worship Him at the first sign of enemy attack and to make that one of your greatest weapons of spiritual warfare, along with God's Word, prayer, and calling on the name of Jesus.

_____

_____

_____

_____

7. Read the following Scriptures. Under each one write out a proclamation of praise and worship inspired by those words.

Psalm 50:14

_____

_____

Psalm 89:5-9

_____

_____

Psalm 95:1-2

_____

_____

Psalm 95:3-5

_____

_____

Psalm 100:1-5

_____

_____

Psalm 134:1-2

_____

_____

Psalm 135:1-3

_____

_____

8. Read Psalm 103:1-2. David said, "Bless the LORD, O my soul, and forget not all His benefits." We often forget God's benefits. When we have a job, we know whether we have benefits from our employer or we don't. That isn't something we forget. *God's* benefits are forever and far greater than any we can ever get from another source, yet too often we forget them.

Below are some of the benefits God gives us. These are the things He does for those who worship Him. Under each Scripture, write out a short prayer praising God for things listed in that verse and ask Him to help you to remember to praise Him for them often.

Psalm 103:3

_____

_____

Psalm 103:4

_____

_____

Psalm 103:5

_____

_____

Psalm 103:6

_____

_____

Psalm 103:7

_____

_____

Psalm 103:8

_____

_____

9. Psalm 116:12-14 and 17 says, "What shall I render to the LORD
    for all His benefits toward me? I will take up the cup of salvation,
    and call upon the name of the LORD. I will pay my vows to the
    LORD now in the presence of all His people...I will offer to You
    the sacrifice of thanksgiving, and will call upon the name of the
    LORD."

    Read Psalm 103:9-18. Write out a short prayer of praise for
    what each verse lists as benefits for you.

Psalm 103:9

_____

_____

_____

Psalm 103:10

_____

_____

_____

Psalm 103:11

_____

_____

_____

Psalm 103:12

_____

_____

_____

Psalm 103:13

_____

_____

_____

Psalm 103:14

_____

_____

_____

Psalm 103:17-18

_____

_____

_____

Read Psalm 78:32-33,42. We show our love for God by remembering what He has done. When the Israelites did not remember what God had done for them, what happened? What did they not remember?

_____

_____

---

10. Pray the prayer on page 143 in the book. Write out several sentences from the prayer that are especially important to you right now. You can write them in the exact words used there or in your own words.

Week Eleven

Read Chapter 11:
"Look for Ways to Trust Him Completely"
in *Choose Love*

~~~~~~

1. Read Proverbs 3:5-6. Write out these verses as a prayer asking God to help you do what is described there. (For example, "Lord, help me to trust in You with…")

   _____

   _____

   _____

   _____

2. Read Psalm 42:5. Is there any serious concern in your life right now about which you must remind yourself to trust in God, put your hope in Him, and praise Him in the face of it? If so, write out a prayer asking God to help you do all that. If you have no immediate concerns, is there something you are worried *could happen* in the future? If so, write out a prayer telling God of your concern and ask Him to help you put your hope completely in Him.

   _____

   _____

_____

_____

3. Read Psalm 91:11-12. How do these verses make you feel with
    regard to trusting God?

_____

_____

_____

Have you ever had an experience where you knew God inter-
vened in your life to spare you—or protect or rescue you or
someone you love—from something serious? Explain.

_____

_____

_____

4. Read the following Scriptures. Under each one write out a
    prayer including all or part of that Scripture. Mention what
    kind of threat, or what specific situation, would cause you to
    include this Scripture in a prayer. (For example, "Lord, I feel
    afraid at night because of dangers I am aware of, so I am thank-
    ful that Your Word says I do not need to be afraid of…")

Psalm 91:5-6

_____

_____

_____

Psalm 91:7-10

_____

_____

_____

Psalm 27:13-14

_____

_____

_____

Psalm 91:14-15

_____

_____

_____

Isaiah 26:3

_____

_____

_____

5. Read Malachi 3:16-18. Many of the people had been complaining harshly against God, saying it was useless to serve Him (3:14). But the people who *feared* God spoke up for Him. So a book of remembrance was written for those who reverenced Him. God recognizes both evil and good behavior. What does God promise to those who trust Him completely?

    _____

    _____

    _____

6. Read Psalm 5:11-12. Why does God give us joy? How does He respond to our love of Him? Write out your answer as a prayer of thanks to God. (For example, "Lord, I thank You that You bring me joy because I...")

    _____

    _____

    _____

    _____

7. Read Psalm 32:10-11. In these verses, what is the promise to those who are evil? What is the promise to those who trust in God?

    _____

    _____

    _____

    _____

8. Read Psalm 4:5. Our obedience is a sacrifice we offer to God when we put our total trust in Him. We show our love for God when we put our complete trust in Him and depend on Him totally. Write out a prayer asking God to help you do what this Scripture says to do.

_____

_____

_____

_____

9. Read the following Scriptures. Under each one write out a prayer of thanks for the reasons you can trust God mentioned in that Scripture. (For example, "Lord, I thank You that I can trust You at all times because You are always my salvation, strength, and…")

Psalm 62:7-8

_____

_____

Psalm 145:19-20

_____

_____

Psalm 91:3-4

_____

_____

Psalm 33:20-21

_____

_____

Matthew 6:33-34

_____

_____

When we trust God in everything we do and don't try to have it all figured out ourselves—when we acknowledge God in every part of our lives—then He will guide us and lead us in the right direction. We will experience life-enhancing opportunities because of walking closely with Him in prayer and trusting Him to answer according to His will. Write out a prayer thanking God for all that.

_____

_____

_____

_____

10. Pray the prayer on page 154 in the book. Write out several sentences from the prayer that are especially important to you right now. You can write them in the exact words used there or in your own words.

_____

_____

_____

_____

Week Twelve

Read Chapter 12:
"Lean on His Wisdom Enthusiastically"
in *Choose Love*

~~~~~~

1. Read Proverbs 2:1-5. How are we to get wisdom? What will we gain when we do that?

    _____

    _____

    _____

    _____

2. Read Proverbs 2:6-9. Where does godly wisdom come from? What does God do for us when we enthusiastically seek His wisdom?

    _____

    _____

    _____

    _____

Read Proverbs 8:17. What assures us that we can receive wisdom from God?

_____

_____

3. Read Proverbs 2:10-14. What happens when wisdom enters your heart? From what does godly wisdom protect you?

_____

_____

_____

_____

4. Proverbs 3:19-26. What happens when you seek and keep godly wisdom in your heart? How will that bring you peace?

_____

_____

_____

_____

5. If God's wisdom founded the earth and heaven, do you believe He can sustain you when you declare your love for Him and your dependence on Him? Why or why not? Write out your answer as a prayer. (For example, "Lord, I pray You will strengthen my faith in Your wisdom because sometimes I am afraid to truly trust it, and...")

_____

_____

_____

_____

6. Read Job 3:24-26. Do you have any concerns that something you greatly fear may happen? What is that? Write out your answer in a prayer telling God of what worries you and ask Him to keep that from happening. (For example, "Lord, I'm very concerned that my nephew, who is deployed in a war zone, may be killed or badly injured, so I pray You will surround him with angels and put Your hand of protection...")

_____

_____

_____

_____

7. Read 1 Corinthians 1:18-25. What is the message of Jesus' death on the cross and His resurrection to those who do not know Him? (verse 18)

_____

_____

What does God say about people who only have worldly wisdom? (verses 19-21)

_____

_____

The message of the cross is foolishness to unbelievers of the world, but what is it to those who believe? (verse 24)

_____

_____

8. What does 1 Corinthians 1:25 say about God regarding foolishness and weakness? How does that make you feel with regard to His wisdom, strength, and power toward you?

_____

_____

_____

_____

9. Read Psalm 111:10 and Proverbs 1:7. Where do true wisdom and knowledge begin in us? Write out your answer as a prayer asking God to give you deep reverence in your heart for Him and the wisdom to live His way.

_____

_____

_____

_____

10. Pray the prayer on page 164 in the book. Write out several sentences from the prayer that are especially important to you right now. You can write them in the exact words used there or in your own words.

_____

_____

_____

_____

Week Thirteen

Read Chapter 13:
"Leave the World of His Enemy Entirely"
in *Choose Love*

~~~~~~

1. Read Psalm 27:4-6. What will God do for us because we choose
    to separate ourselves from the enemy and dwell with the Lord?
    What do we need to offer to Him?

    _____

    _____

    _____

    _____

2. Read Ezra 10:11. Because the "peoples of the land" were ene-
    mies of God, what did He ask the children of Israel to do? In
    light of that, what is one thing we can do to show our love for
    God?

    _____

    _____

    _____

    _____

3. Read Psalm 18:37-40. In these verses, David was persistent in removing his enemies from his life. Do you feel you can be as persistent until you no longer allow the enemy into any part of your life? How so?

_____

_____

_____

_____

Write down the five subheads in this chapter as a reminder list for yourself. (See pages 168, 169, 172, 174, and 175 in the book.)

1. _____

_____

2. _____

_____

3. _____

_____

4. _____

_____

5. _____

_____

4. Read Psalm 135:13-18. What do these verses say about having idols in our life?

_____

_____

_____

5. Write out a prayer asking God to reveal to you any idols in your life. We normally don't think of ourselves as having idols because we don't have anything like a calf made of gold sitting in our house, but when we seek God about it, it's surprising what He may point out.

_____

_____

_____

_____

Write down anything the Lord shows you and ask Him to set you free from anything He doesn't want you to love more than Him.

_____

_____

_____

_____

6. Read Psalm 11:1-3. What do you think we, the righteous, can do to establish ourselves on a firm foundation in the Lord? What happens when we don't?

_____

_____

_____

_____

7. Read Psalm 30:1-2. Why did David praise God?

_____

_____

_____

_____

Read Psalm 31:1-5. What did David ask of God?

_____

_____

_____

_____

8. Read Psalm 18:33-36. What does God do for you when you separate yourself from all evil and cling to the Lord for your life?

_____

_____

_____

_____

9. Read Psalm 37:37-40. Write out these verses as a prayer thanking God for all He will do for you when you separate yourself from the evil of the enemy.

_____

_____

_____

_____

Read Psalm 37:9. Write out a prayer of thanks to God for the truth in this verse.

_____

_____

_____

Read Psalm 17:8-9, Psalm 31:14, and Psalm 141:8-10. Write out a prayer that prays these same things for you.

_____

_____

_____

_____

10. Pray the prayer on page 177 in the book. Write out several sentences from the prayer that are especially important to you right now. You can write them in the exact words used there or in your own words.

_____

_____

_____

_____

Week Fourteen

Read Chapter 14:
"Long for His Will and His Presence Continuously"
in *Choose Love*

1. Read Psalm 42:1-2. Have you felt like this in your heart about the Lord? Have you ever longed for His presence even more than food or water? Describe what you have felt with regard to God.

    _____

    _____

    _____

    _____

2. Read John 4:34. What did Jesus say was His food?

    _____

    _____

    _____

3. Read Romans 12:2. In light of this Scripture, what do you need to do? What will happen when you do that?

    _____

    _____

    _____

    _____

4. Read Ephesians 5:17. What do we need in order to do God's will? Write out your answer as a prayer asking God to help you do that. (For example, "Lord, I pray You will help me to be…")

    _____

    _____

    _____

    _____

5. Read John 6:39-40. What was the will of God that Jesus came to fulfill?

    _____

    _____

    _____

    _____

6. What do you believe is God's will for you? Write out a prayer asking God to show you more about that and help you fulfill His will in your life. If you don't yet have a sense of what His will is, write out a prayer asking Him to show you in some way what

His purpose is for you. Then write down whatever He shows you and ask Him to help you to do that. (For example, "Lord, I want to know what Your will is for my life, so I ask You to show me…")

_____

_____

_____

_____

7. Read Psalm 107:10-14. Living outside of God's will is rebellion against Him and His Word. What happens when people do that?

    _____

    _____

    _____

    What happens when people wholeheartedly cry out to the Lord in repentance?

    _____

    _____

    _____

8. When we understand the will of God, we have true wisdom. When we seek to live in the will of God, we are wise. Human wisdom is full of pride and arrogance, but when we seek the wisdom of God, we are humble. It means that we glory in the Lord

and not in ourselves. Write out a prayer asking God to help you do His will in everything so that you can always glorify Him.

_____

_____

_____

_____

9. Read Psalm 27:4. What did David want most?

_____

_____

Read Psalm 140:13. What does this Scripture say about the people who live God's way?

_____

_____

In light of the two verses above, write out a prayer telling God how you feel about living your life in His presence as much as is possible on this earth. (For example, "Lord, I want to live in Your presence more than anything else, so I ask that You would help me to…") (Or, "Lord, help me to understand how to live in Your will and Your presence because I know it's there I will find…")

_____

_____

_____

_____

10. Pray the prayer on page 188 in the book. Write out several sentences from the prayer that are especially important to you right now. You can write them in the exact words used there or in your own words.

_____

_____

_____

_____

Third Choice

Choose to Love Others in a Way That Pleases God

Week Fifteen

Read Chapter 15:
"Is Consistently Loving Others Really Possible?"
in *Choose Love*

~~~~~~

1. Read 1 John 4:8. How is consistently loving others possible? If we have a hard time loving others, what do we need to do?

_____

_____

_____

_____

2. Read Romans 5:5. How do we receive more of the love of God in us?

_____

_____

_____

3. Read 1 John 4:14-16. What is true of anyone who receives Jesus as God's Son and Savior? What is true of us because we believe in and receive the love God has for us?

_____

_____

_____

_____

4. Read John 13:34-35. What is the new commandment Jesus gave us? Why does He want us to do that? How important is it to you to do what Jesus asks of you?

_____

_____

_____

_____

5. Read John 15:9-13. What does Jesus ask us to do? (verse 9)

_____

_____

What does Jesus want you to do and why? (verses 10-11)

_____

_____

What is His commandment? (verse 12)

_____

_____

What is His greatest act of love? (verse 13)

_____

_____

6. Read 1 John 4:20. What is true of us if we don't love others? How important is it to not be perceived that way by God or people? Why?

_____

_____

_____

_____

7. Read John 15:14-17. What must you do to be a friend of Jesus? (verse 14)

_____

_____

Why does He not call those who serve Him "servants"? (verse 15)

_____

_____

What does He promise to do? (verse 16)

_____

_____

What does He command us to do? (verse 17)

_____

_____

8. Read 1 Thessalonians 3:12-13. God can establish our hearts as
    blameless when we love others. Write out a prayer asking God
    to do that in you just as Paul prayed for the Thessalonians.

    _____

    _____

    _____

    _____

9. We are capable of kind acts, but we are not capable of consis-
    tently loving others the way God loves us without His love *in* us.
    Write out a prayer asking God to pour His Spirit of love afresh
    in you every day and give you the ability to love others the way
    He loves you.

    _____

    _____

    _____

    _____

10. Pray the prayer on page 202 in the book. Write out several sentences from the prayer that are especially important to you right now. You can write them in the exact words used there or in your own words.

_____

_____

_____

_____

Week Sixteen

Read Chapter 16:
"What if I Can't Always Be Patient and Kind?"
in *Choose Love*

~~~~~~

1. Read Psalm 86:15. What does this verse say about the character and nature of God? What are the words that describe Him?

_____

_____

_____

_____

2. Read Titus 3:3-7. What do these verses say about the nature of Jesus? What are the words that describe Him?

_____

_____

_____

_____

3. Read 1 Timothy 1:14-16. What did Paul say about Jesus with regard to himself? In what way do you identify with those words in regard to yourself?

_____

_____

_____

_____

4. Can you think of a specific time where you have suffered long? Is there a person in your life right now you can think of with whom you have been doing that? Write out a prayer for that situation or person, asking God to give you the kind of love and patience in your heart that enables you to continue to bear with that person without becoming bitter or unforgiving. Ask God to show you what you are to *keep* doing or *stop* doing.

_____

_____

_____

_____

5. Is there someone in your life now, or in your past, who has been painfully impatient with you? Is it still hurtful to this day, or have you been able to completely forgive him or her? Either way, write out a prayer asking God to help you completely forgive that person and the incident or incidents. Remember, we need the love of God in us and the help of the Holy Spirit in order to

do this. Ask God to take away all the hurt and bad feelings and enable you to let it go completely.

_____

_____

_____

_____

6. Read Ephesians 4:1-2. What did Paul ask believers to do?

_____

_____

_____

_____

Write out a prayer asking God to show you who He wants you to be especially patient with right now. Ask Him to fill you with His patience and enable you to be kind in that situation.

_____

_____

_____

_____

7. Read Colossians 1:9-11. Write out these verses as a prayer for yourself. (For example, "Lord, I pray I will be filled with the knowledge of Your will...")

_____

_____

_____

_____

Now write out these verses as a prayer for someone you know who especially needs it. (For example, "Lord, I pray for [name or initials of person] to be filled with wisdom and spiritual understanding and knowledge of Your will so that…")

_____

_____

_____

_____

8. Consistently being patient and kind to the degree God wants us to be is impossible on our own; it's only possible when we open up to His love for us. His love is the extreme example of patience and kindness. When we express *our* love for *Him*, He fills *us* with *His* love. Read the other words for "patient" in the book on page 206, the last full paragraph to the top half of page 207. Write out a prayer asking God to enable you to be what these words are describing. Go through and pick out the words you feel you need the most help becoming. Don't worry. Only God can enable us to be any of these things.

_____

_____

_____

_____

9. Read Psalm 63:3-4. What do these verses say about God's nature? What are we to do in response to that?

_____

_____

_____

_____

Read the other words for "kind" on page 211 in the book, the third paragraph through page 212. Write out a prayer asking God to help you be those things. Choose a few of the words you know you need the most help becoming, and ask Him to show you which one you most need His help to accomplish right now, keeping in mind we all need His help with each one of them. Just do what you can handle right now.

_____

_____

_____

_____

10. Pray the prayer on page 213 in the book. Write out several sentences from the prayer that are especially important to you right now. You can write them in the exact words used there or in your own words.

_____

_____

_____

_____

Week Seventeen

Read Chapter 17:
"In What Ways Do I Reveal a Lack of Love?"
in *Choose Love*

〜〜〜〜〜〜〜〜〜〜〜〜〜〜〜〜〜〜〜〜〜〜〜〜〜〜

1. Read 1 Corinthians 13:4-6. The eight subheads in the corresponding chapter in the book talk about the ways we can reveal a lack of love in ourselves. The first one is on page 215. What is listed in the first subhead that love does not do? Complete the following sentence: Love does not...

    _____

    _____

    What are some other words and phrases for "envy"? (See page 217 in the book, first paragraph.) Which ones especially speak to you as feelings you want to avoid? Write out your answer as a prayer asking God to help you be so full of His love that you never have any of those feelings toward others.

    _____

    _____

    _____

    _____

2. See page 217, bottom of the page. The second way we can reveal a lack of love for others is...

_____

_____

Have you ever done that and felt bad about it? Or have you seen others do that and felt uncomfortable around them? Describe the situation and how you felt.

_____

_____

_____

_____

Read the list of other words and phrases describing "parading ourselves" on page 218, third paragraph, and then list which ones you most want God to keep you from ever doing. Write out your answer as a prayer asking God to help you never do those things.

_____

_____

_____

_____

3. See page 219 in the book. The third way we can reveal a lack of love in us is...

_____

_____

Have you ever been that way? Have you seen others be that way? How did that make you feel?

_____

_____

_____

_____

In the lists of other words and phrases for "puffed up" and "prideful" at the bottom of page 219 and the top of page 220, which words stand out to you that you most want to avoid in yourself? Write your answer out as a prayer asking God to keep you from ever being that way.

_____

_____

_____

_____

4. See the middle of page 220. The fourth way we can reveal a lack of love for others is...

_____

_____

Have you ever done that or observed someone else acting that way? Describe how it made you feel.

_____

_____

_____

_____

In the list of words and phrases for "rude" at the bottom of page 220 and the top of page 221, which ones do you most want God to help you avoid being? Write out a prayer asking Him to keep you from any kind of action like that.

_____

_____

_____

_____

5. See page 221. The fifth way we can reveal a lack of love in us is...

_____

_____

We all have a tendency to be that way. How would you rate yourself with this? (See the first three paragraphs under the subhead on selfishness.)

_____

_____

_____

_____

In the list of other words and phrases for "seeking its own" in the last two paragraphs on page 221 and the top of page 222, which are the ones you most want God to keep you from being?

Write out your answer as a prayer asking Him to enable you to never do any of these specific things.

_____

_____

_____

_____

6. See page 222. The sixth way we can reveal a lack of love is…

_____

_____

Have you ever been that way, or are you now, or are you close to someone who is that way? Describe the situation and how it makes you feel.

_____

_____

_____

_____

In the list of other words and phrases for "provoked" in the last two paragraphs of page 222, which ones are you most concerned about, either for yourself or for someone close to you? Write out your answer as a prayer asking God to enable you to avoid that in yourself or open another person's eyes to it in themselves.

_____

_____

_____

_____

7. See page 223. The seventh way we can reveal a lack of love in us is…

_____

_____

Describe what people who think bad thoughts are like. (See the first two paragraphs under the subhead.)

_____

_____

_____

_____

In the list of other words for "guile," what are the ones that most stand out to you as ones you want God to help you avoid? (See the third and fourth paragraphs under the subtitle.) Write out your answer as a prayer asking God to keep you from ever being like that.

_____

_____

_____

_____

8. See page 224. The eighth way we can reveal a lack of love in ourselves is…

   _____

   _____

   Describe what that means.

   _____

   _____

   _____

   _____

   In the list of other words and phrases for "iniquity" in the last
   two paragraphs on page 224 and top of page 225, which words
   stand out to you most as ones you want to avoid in yourself?
   Write out your answer as a prayer asking God to help you do that.

   _____

   _____

   _____

   _____

9. Read Proverbs 14:12 and the last two paragraphs on page 225
   in the book. Write out a prayer asking God to help you never
   show a lack of love in any way. Tell Him you don't want to pay
   the consequences for that lapse in judgment. Pray for someone
   else who needs prayer in that regard as well.

   _____

   _____

_____

_____

10. Pray the prayer on page 226 in the book. Write out several sentences from the prayer that are especially important to you right now. You can write them in the exact words used there or in your own words.

_____

_____

_____

_____

Week Eighteen

Read Chapter 18:
"How Will Others Know I Am God's?"
in *Choose Love*

~~~~~~

1. Read Ephesians 4:1-3. What does God want us to do with regard to others?

   _____

   _____

   _____

   _____

2. Read 1 Peter 4:8. What are we to do and why?

   _____

   _____

   _____

   _____

3. Read 1 Thessalonians 3:12. Write out this prayer Paul prayed for the Thessalonians as a prayer for yourself.

   _____

   _____

_____

_____

4. Read Matthew 25:34-40. What is your greatest motivation for
   showing love for others? What happens when you care sacrifi-
   cially for other people?

   _____

   _____

   _____

   _____

5. On our own, we don't have the depth of love that is described
   in God's Word as the way love *should* be. We have to pray to
   be filled with *His* love so that we can extend it to others. Every
   time we show love to a person, it brings healing of some kind
   to us and to our relationship. We cannot neglect to do that for
   the people in our lives who are closest to us—family and friends
   whom we love. Sometimes these relationships can become frag-
   ile because we take them for granted and do not pray for them as
   we should, or we get busy and don't take the time to express our
   love toward them. That's why it is good to pray often for each
   person and relationship and ask God to show us who needs a
   special expression of love from us right then.
       Write out a prayer asking God to help you show His love
   to the people closest to you, lifting them up to Him by name,
   and ask Him who especially needs an expression of love from
   you right now.

   _____

   _____

_____

_____

6. Write out a prayer asking God to show you who else around you especially needs to be shown love right now. Write down the name of anyone He brings to mind. (It may be someone you wouldn't have thought of if He hadn't prompted you.)

_____

_____

_____

_____

7. Ask God to help you be a "Repairer of the Breach" (Isaiah 58:12). Families are grieved when a breach exists between members and one person pulls away from another, sometimes causing others to take sides. And these people perpetuate that hurt in the family so that the pain is always felt. It's a pain that doesn't heal because the love of God is never fully extended. Or it is extended by one person, but the other person refuses to receive it.

Let me be clear—I am not talking about when abuse is happening and the person must get away from the abuser. Not enabling an abuser to keep on sinning is actually a loving thing to do. I am talking about petty disagreements where someone's feelings were hurt and that person doesn't communicate about their hurt for the purpose of forgiveness and reconciliation, but rather wants to continuously punish the offending person by their unforgiveness. Or where the person who hurt the feelings of another refuses to ask forgiveness for doing that.

People have to *choose* to show the love of God in order for reconciliation to happen. But too often they choose to continue to perpetuate the grievance and grieve God also. Write out a prayer asking God to help you be one who brings healing and reconciliation to relationships that have broken down, whether it is between others only or others and you.

_____

_____

_____

_____

8. Read 1 Peter 1:22. What are we supposed to do?

_____

_____

_____

Read Hebrews 10:24. How do we inspire others to do good?

_____

_____

_____

9. Read 1 John 3:10. How do we communicate to others who it is we serve?

_____

_____

_____

Read 1 John 3:14-17. What does it reveal about us when we love others? (verse 14)

_____

_____

_____

What does it say of people who hate others? (verse 15)

_____

_____

_____

How do we know love? (verse 16)

_____

_____

_____

What does it say of us when we don't help others in need? (verse 17)

_____

_____

_____

10. Pray the prayer on page 234 in the book. Write out several sentences from the prayer that are especially important to you right

now. You can write them in the exact words used there or in your own words.

_____

_____

_____

_____

Week Nineteen

Read Chapter 19:
"Isn't It Selfish to Learn to Love Myself?"
in *Choose Love*

~~~~~~

1. Read Galatians 5:14. What are you supposed to do?

    _____

    _____

    _____

    If you do not love yourself, how well will you love others?

    _____

    _____

    _____

2. Read James 2:8. How do you fulfill the royal law?

    _____

    _____

    _____

How well can you do that if you don't love yourself?

_____

_____

3. Read 1 Corinthians 6:19-20. Why should you love and appreciate who God made you to be? (See page 239 in the book, the first two paragraphs.)

_____

_____

_____

_____

4. Read Psalm 19:14. Write out this prayer of David as a prayer for yourself to keep you from saying bad things or thinking critical thoughts about yourself.

_____

_____

_____

_____

5. What are your thoughts about yourself? Do you appreciate the person God has made you to be? Do you trust Him to do great things in you and in your life? Why or why not?

_____

_____

_____

_____

6. Have there been any incidents or times in your life when you
    disliked or hated yourself? If so, confess them to God and ask
    Him to help you love and appreciate who He created you to be.
    If not, write out a prayer thanking God for who He made you
    to be. Either way, include in your prayer specific things about
    yourself for which you are especially grateful. (This list is very
    important and can be added to as God brings things to mind.)

    _____

    _____

    _____

    _____

7. Do you tend to be hard on yourself? Confess that to the Lord
    in a prayer asking Him to help you see yourself as He sees you.

    _____

    _____

    _____

    _____

8. Read the bottom of page 241 and first two paragraphs of page
    242 in the book. Write out a prayer listing the bad thoughts you
    tend to think about yourself and ask God to help you to be rid

of those thoughts by replacing them with *His* thoughts about you.

_____

_____

_____

_____

9. Read Psalm 118:23-24. Write out these verses as a prayer about yourself that you can pray whenever you find you are thinking critical thoughts about yourself.

_____

_____

_____

_____

Read the rest of page 242 in the book and the first four lines at the top of page 243. Write out a prayer asking God to help you see all the good things about your life. Then thank Him for all of those things specifically.

_____

_____

_____

_____

10. Pray the prayer on page 244 in the book. Write out several sentences from the prayer that are especially important to you right now. You can write them in the exact words used there or in your own words.

_____

_____

_____

_____

Week Twenty

Read Chapter 20:
"What if I'm Unable to Bear,
Believe, Hope, and Endure All Things?"
in *Choose Love*

~~~~~~

1. Read Colossians 3:12-13 and Ephesians 4:13. Is there any place
    in your life where you are having trouble *bearing* or putting up
    with something or someone in your life? Complete the follow-
    ing sentence: I am having difficulty bearing, tolerating, or put-
    ting up with…

    _____

    _____

    Write out a prayer asking God to help you bear up under what
    you are facing. Ask Him to take the problem away or show
    you what to do about it. Most of all, ask Him to help you rely
    totally on His strength.

    _____

    _____

    _____

    _____

2. Read the other words and phrases for "bear" on the bottom of page 248 and the top of page 249. What words most stand out to you that you want God to help you do or not do? Write out your answer as a prayer asking Him to help you *do* or *not* do that.

    _____

    _____

    _____

    _____

3. Read Matthew 21:22. Is there any place in your life where you are having a hard time *believing* for the best? Complete the following sentence: I'm having a hard time right now believing that...

    _____

    _____

    Write out a prayer asking God to strengthen your faith in His desire and ability to answer your prayers, and then pray about this specific situation.

    _____

    _____

    _____

    _____

4. Read the other words and phrases for "believe" on page 249. What words do you most want God to help you do or not do?

Write out your answer as a prayer asking Him to help you *do* or *not* do that.

_____

_____

_____

_____

5. Read Romans 8:24-25 and Psalm 31:24. Is there any area or situation in your life where you are losing *hope* or you feel you have lost all hope? Complete the following sentence: I feel I have lost or am losing hope regarding...

_____

_____

Write out a prayer confessing that you are having a struggle being hopeful about this situation, and ask God to help you remember it is Christ in you who gives you hope.

_____

_____

_____

_____

6. Read the other words and phrases for "hope" on page 250. What words stand out to you that you most want God to help you do or not do? Write out your answer as a prayer asking Him to help you *do* or *not* do that.

_____

_____

_____

_____

7. Read Hebrews 12:3. Who endured hostility and torture for you?

_____

_____

Why do you need to remember that?

_____

_____

Complete this sentence: I feel I can no longer *endure*...

_____

_____

_____

Write out a prayer asking God to either give you relief from what you are enduring or strengthen you to go through it. Thank Him for all He endured for you out of love, and because of that you, too, can endure what He allows you to go through out of love for others.

_____

_____

_____

_____

8. Read the other words and phrases for "endure" on the bottom of page 250 and the top of page 251. What words do you most want God to help you do or not do? Write out your answer as a prayer asking Him to help you *do* or *not* do that.

    _____

    _____

    _____

    _____

9. Read Hebrews 6:15. This Scripture is talking about Abraham. In what manner was he required to endure? What did he gain by doing so?

    _____

    _____

    _____

    _____

    Write out a prayer asking God to help you clearly understand what He is requiring of you and to enable you to do it. Thank Him for the promises in His Word you will receive because of doing what He asks you to do.

    _____

    _____

    _____

    _____

10. Pray the prayer on page 252 in the book. Write out several sentences from the prayer that are especially important to you right now. You can write them in the exact words used there or in your own words.

_____

_____

_____

_____

Week Twenty-One

Read Chapter 21:
"How Can I Show Love in Every Situation?"
in *Choose Love*

︿︿︿︿︿︿︿︿︿︿︿︿︿︿︿︿︿︿︿︿︿

1. Read 1 Corinthians 13:13. Why do you think love is the greatest of the three virtues listed here? (See page 255 in the book.)

   _____

   _____

   _____

   _____

2. Read 2 Corinthians 6:3-8. Describe in your own words how Paul conducted his life in the Lord.

   _____

   _____

   _____

   _____

3. Just as God is real, so is His love. That's because God *is* love. That's who He is. Without Him there is no love that heals,

restores, draws, delivers, and resurrects. Write out a prayer asking God to pour His love into you so you can show the kind of love that brings healing and restoration to others and draws them to Him.

_____

_____

_____

_____

4. Read 2 Peter 1:5-8. Write out a prayer asking God to help you add these things to your faith. Thank Him for the blessings promised to you when you do.

_____

_____

_____

_____

5. Read Proverbs 5:21. What does this Scripture speak to you about showing love to others?

_____

_____

_____

6. Read Proverbs 17:9. Write out a prayer asking God to help you always show love with the words you speak—that there may never be any spreading of gossip or loveless words about another.

Confess any words you wish you had never said so you can be forgiven for them.

_____

_____

_____

_____

7. Read 2 Thessalonians 2:16-17. Write these verses out as a prayer for yourself. (For example, "Lord, I pray that You, who loves me and gives me grace and hope for eternity, would...")

_____

_____

_____

_____

8. Read Proverbs 17:17. Write out a prayer asking God to help you be a loving friend at all times.

_____

_____

_____

_____

9. Read Proverbs 17:22. I have always read this proverb as a reminder to keep a cheerful heart because it was vital to my health. But after the revelation God gave me about love in 1 Corinthians 13, I saw this Scripture with new eyes. I saw that

my merry heart does good for others like a medicine too. The capacity to laugh is good for others as well as for us. That doesn't mean we *pretend* to be happy and become phony in that respect. It means we find our joy in the Lord every day and let it pour out of us as a blessing to others without losing our sensitivity to their pain and suffering. Write out a prayer asking God to give you a joyful heart that speaks love to others and helps to heal those who have a broken spirit.

_____

_____

_____

_____

10. Pray the prayer on page 261 in the book. Write out several sentences from the prayer that are especially important to you right now. You can write them in the exact words used there or in your own words.

_____

_____

_____

_____

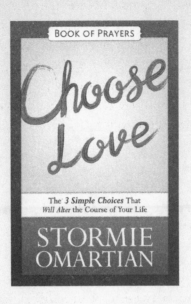

Every day, do you receive God's great love for you, express that back to Him, and then share it with others? That kind of power—the power of His amazing loving-kindness shown toward you—can transform your life and the lives of those around you. It brings you into a deeper relationship with God as well as with people, and that gives you greater peace.

Let this little book of prayers help you be a person who loves well. Also included are encouraging Scriptures and a space for notes and thoughts and prayers of your own.

You can be the gift to the world *around* you that God wants to give *through* you. Don't hesitate to choose love.